Golden Footsteps

by

Diana Cooper

Copyright © Diana Cooper 1996

First published 1996

ISBN 1 899171 71 1

British Library Cataloguing-in-Publication Data.
A catalogue record for this book is available from the British Library.

Cover design and book layout by David Gregson.

Cover photograph © Le Pixel 1994
Printed and bound by C&C Offset, Hong Kong.

Published by
Findhorn Press
The Park, Findhorn, Forres IV36 0TZ, Scotland
tel +44 (0)1309 690582 • fax 690036 • email thierry@findhorn.org
http://www.gaia.org/findhornpress/

THE TREE STOOD TALL AND FIRM. ITS ROOTS WERE ANCHORED DEEP INTO THE EARTH. ITS BRANCHES REACHED TO THE HEAVENS.

I heard the Voice say...

"Be like that tree with your feet on the ground and your head in the stars. Be a link between Heaven and Earth."

I SAW MANY BACK PACKERS AT THE STATION.
SOME HAD TRAVELLED FOR MANY MONTHS WITHOUT
WORKING. I HAD ALWAYS WORKED HARD AND
I JUDGED THEM HARSHLY.

I heard the Voice say…

*"Never judge another's Path. Blessed are they
who travel, for they seek to experience more of
My creation."*

I FELT HARSH AND UNCHARITABLE TOWARDS A COLLEAGUE AT WORK. WHY SHOULD I BE NICE TO HIM, I THOUGHT UNKINDLY.

I heard the Voice say...

"When you do a kindness to another you do it to Me for I am in everyone. All that you give Me I return to you – so be kind to others and I will reward you."

In front of me was a dark, ugly prison wall. I felt gloom and despair as I saw it. And then I noticed a little flower clinging to the wall, its petals wide open and beautiful.

I heard the Voice say…

"My Beauty is everywhere to remind you of My presence. Look for it and know there is hope in the darkest situation."

4

I SAT IN A CROWD OF MISERABLE PEOPLE AND FELT

GREYNESS CREEP LIKE A MANTLE OVER ME.

I heard the Voice say…

"When you are amongst sad or gloomy people, smile. When you smile it is like lighting a candle in the dark. So open your heart and smile. Spread My Light to everyone."

5

I LOOKED AT THE ENDLESS ROLLING TARMAC PAVEMENTS AND ROADS COVERING ALL THE PLACES WHICH HAD ONCE BEEN GREEN GRASS. THERE GROWING DEFIANTLY THROUGH THE TARMAC WAS A LILY OF THE VALLEY FLOWER. I LEANT DOWN TO SMELL ITS FRAGRANCE AND THAT FRAGRANCE STAYED WITH ME THROUGH THE DAY.

I heard the Voice say...

"Man needs nature and nature does not need man."

THERE SEEMED TO BE TOO MANY PROBLEMS AND
CHALLENGES IN MY LIFE AND I COMPLAINED AND
GRUMBLED AS I RESISTED THEM ALL.

I heard the Voice say...

"*Do not groan when you are presented with Life's
tests. You must learn from each test and be strengthened
by it. This is the way to gain spiritual promotion so that
you can do more important work.*"

7

My MIND WAS FULL OF DOUBT AND CONFUSION. I DID NOT KNOW WHAT TO DO.

I heard the Voice say...

"When you are in doubt ask. I always reply to you. Know this and keep yourself open for the reply. I may bring it to you in words you glance at, a voice you overhear, a broadcast you catch. So that you may know I am in everyone I may bring your answer through someone you despise. Just listen."

I WORRIED ABOUT PROMOTION AND BUYING A
BETTER CAR. I WANTED MORE EXPENSIVE CLOTHES.

I heard the Voice say…

"*Do not waste your life in seeking material possessions. They are nothing but material possessions. They perish. Spend your life in acquiring experience, knowledge, wisdom and in seeking Truth. They will be yours through eternity.*"

9

I YEARNED FOR THE SWIMMING POOL TO BE CLEAR
AND PURE AND VERY PEACEFUL. AS I CLEANED
IT OUT I REALISED JUST HOW MUCH WORK THIS
WOULD MEAN.

I heard the Voice say…

*"I will help you to cleanse the pool within you
so that your thoughts are pure. Then you will have a
beautiful pool of peace within"*

10

My FRIEND TAUGHT HIS LITTLE GIRLS TO HUG
TREES. EVERY WEEK THEY WALKED ON THE HILL
NEAR THEIR HOME AND HUGGED CERTAIN TREES.
THEN GALES CAME AND DEVASTATED THAT PART OF
THE COUNTRY. WHEN MY FRIEND AND HIS LITTLE
GIRLS WENT BACK TO THE HILL AFTER THE GALES
THEY FOUND THAT ONLY THE TREES THEY HAD
HUGGED REMAINED STANDING. THEY WONDERED IF
THEIR HUGS HAD SAVED THOSE TREES.

I heard the Voice say...

*"Love is the most powerful force on Earth.
The strength it gives helps to withstand all adversity."*

11

THE CHILD HAD TWISTED FEET AND HER PARENTS
WERE TOLD SHE WOULD NEVER WALK. BUT THEY
LOVINGLY MASSAGED HER FEET FOR HOURS EACH DAY
UNTIL THEY BECAME STRAIGHT AND STRONG.
THEN THE CHILD WALKED.

I heard the Voice say...

*"When you do something for another with love you
bestow My Grace on them. Love heals others."*

12

THE TREE WAS A HUGE ANCIENT YEW. FEELING
SMALL AND INSIGNIFICANT, I HESITATED BEFORE
I DREW CLOSE TO IT TO TOUCH IT.

I heard the Voice say...

*"Come close. My strength is always available to
you to draw on."*

...AND A CLOAK OF WARMTH AND PEACE
ENVELOPED ME.

13

I WATCHED A ROW OF BABY BIRDS ON THE BRANCH. THEY FLUTTERED THEIR WINGS BUT WERE AFRAID TO FLY. THEY HUNG ONTO THE BRANCH UNTIL THE PARENT BIRDS PUSHED THEM OFF. AND ONE BY ONE THEY REALISED THAT WHEN THEY LET GO, THEY COULD FLY. THEY WERE FREE.

I heard the Voice say…

"When you let go and trust yourself to Me, you will fly. The freedom of the Universe will be yours".

14

I WORKED HARD FOR MONEY IN THE BANK AND A PENSION TO MAKE ME FEEL SAFE AND SECURE BUT THERE WAS NEVER ENOUGH.

I heard the Voice say...

"Wealth does not lie in gold, nor security in a big bank balance. These can be taken away from you in a moment. True wealth, true security lie in attuning to Me every moment. I will fill you with faith which no man can take away."

15

THE GARDENER PRUNED SO MUCH DEAD WOOD OUT OF THE BUSH THAT IT LOOKED VULNERABLE AND EXPOSED. BY THE FOLLOWING SPRING IT WAS STRONG, ALIVE AND FULL OF NEW GROWTH.

I heard the Voice say...

"*It is time to prune the old from your life. Prune out old beliefs and patterns, negative people and unhelpful situations. You may feel vulnerable and exposed for a while but then you will become strong and alive. New growth will accelerate within you.*"

16

I WATCHED THE SMALL CHILD UNWRAP THE GIFT HIS PARENTS HAD LOVINGLY PREPARED. THE CHILD'S FACE GLOWED WITH JOY. HE SAID, "THANK YOU," FROM HIS HEART. I KNEW HIS PARENTS WOULD HAVE GIVEN HIM ALL THEY HAD, THEY LOVED HIM SO MUCH.

I heard the Voice say…

"And when you thank Me from your heart for My gifts to you, I love you so much I would give you all."

It was a dark grey, windy night. I was lost in the woods and the trees were black and forbidding. I stumbled frightened in the dark, feeling cold and tired. All at once I saw a light ahead – a cottage light. My energy renewed by hope I hurried towards it.

I heard the Voice say…

"*When you are a Light for Me, you can guide the steps of those who are lost and give them hope when they are tired.*"

I SAW IN FRONT OF ME A BARREN CONCRETE BLOCK OF APARTMENTS. I SEARCHED THE WALLS FOR A SIGN OF LIFE AND AT LAST SAW A BEAUTIFUL, TENACIOUS FLOWER SEEMINGLY GROWING WITHOUT SOIL, CLINGING TO THAT BARE WALL.

I heard the Voice say...

"I am Life. I am in beauty. I am everywhere. Always look for Me."

19

THE ANCIENT LADY WAS WRINKLED AND SENILE. SHE NO LONGER KNEW WHO I WAS, NOR WHERE SHE WAS. HER MIND WAS VAGUE. HER CHATTER EMPTY. "WHAT IS THE PURPOSE OF HER LIFE?" I CRIED.

I heard the Voice say...

"Now she lives with her heart open, loving as her mind never allowed her to do. She is learning to love with simplicity. If you could see her heart now you would rejoice with Me."

20

I LOOKED AT THE TABLE SPREAD WITH RICH AND TEMPTING FOOD.

I heard the Voice say...

"Choose wisely. Eat simply. Your body is a temple to house your spirit. When a temple is beautiful and healthy many are attracted to its vibration for they can find Me there."

21

I LOOKED IN THE MARKET FOR A SMALL WOODEN BOX AND FOUND A CHEAP MASS PRODUCED ONE THAT WOULD FULFIL MY PURPOSE. ON THE NEXT STALL THERE WAS FOR SALE A SMALL, BEAUTIFUL BOX WHICH HAD BEEN LOVINGLY CRAFTED. IT WAS MUCH MORE EXPENSIVE.

I heard the Voice say...

"*When something is made with love and care, the love permeates each cell. Wherever that object is placed for the rest of its life, it radiates that love for all to feel.*"

22

Two PEOPLE WERE GLOWERING AT EACH OTHER. THEIR MOOD WAS DARK AND UGLY.

I heard the Voice say...

"*When you send angry, hurting or lustful thoughts to another, dark shadowy shapes fly from you to that person. When you send love to another, a great rainbow of Light flows between you. It is more beautiful than you can imagine and I rejoice to see it. Focus on loving others and increase the radiance of My world.*"

23

I WATCHED THE MAN RELEASE HIS HOMING PIGEONS,
SOME DARK, SOME WHITE, SOME WEAK, SOME STRONG
– AND THEY ALL FLEW OUT OF SIGHT. LATER I
WATCHED EVERY SINGLE ONE OF THEM COME HOME.

I heard the Voice say...

"Your thoughts and actions too come home. Whatever you think and do eventually comes back to you in some way. So think beautiful, generous, loving thoughts. Do kind and noble actions and know that your life will be filled with beauty, abundance and love."

24

I STRODE AND RACED. I WAS DETERMINED TO BE THE FIRST TO THE TOP OF THE MOUNTAIN. AND I WAS. I WAITED, HOT AND PANTING, FOR THE OTHERS. THEY ARRIVED RELAXED AND SMILING. THEY TALKED OF THE FLOWERS THEY HAD SEEN, OF THE BIRDS THEY HAD HEARD, OF THE PEOPLE THEY HAD SPOKEN TO. I HAD NOTHING TO SHARE.

I heard the Voice say...

"Enjoy each step of your journey, my friend. There is much to experience if you take the time and trouble to look."

25

I WAS PROUD OF MY CHILD. TO MAKE HIM CLEVERER
AND TRY HARDER I REMINDED HIM OF ALL HIS FAULTS
SO HE WOULD LEARN QUICKLY. STRANGELY HE GREW
QUIET AND DULL AND WITHDRAWN.

I heard the Voice say...

*"Love your child and constantly tell him of his good
points. Encourage him with praise."*

SO I LOOKED ONLY FOR HIS GOOD QUALITIES.
AS I PRAISED THEM MY CHILD GREW BRIGHT
AND CLEVER AND JOYOUS. I WAS PROUD OF HIM
AND I LOVED HIM.

26

I LOVED ALL THE BRIGHT, BEAUTIFUL FLOWERS OF THE SUMMER. I DID NOT EVEN NOTICE THE DAISY. ON A COLD, MISTY NOVEMBER DAY THE GARDEN WAS BARE. THERE WERE NO PERFUMED ROSES, NO COLOURFUL ANNUALS. YET THERE IN THE GRASS GREW A DAISY, ITS CENTRE GOLDEN, ITS PETALS WHITE TIPPED WITH PINK.

I heard the Voice say...

"Love is like the daisy – beautiful and modest. It pops up where you least expect it and nothing can stop it spreading"

"**W**HY?" I ASKED. "WHAT IS THE PURPOSE OF LIFE?"

I heard the Voice say…

"*Imagine a family with many children. As they grow up they go out into the world. They grow, expand, learn and mature. When the time is right they feel the call to go Home. Their parents welcome them wholeheartedly no matter what they have done. The experience they have gained and brought back to share enriches the parents too. And in the same way I welcome you back wholeheartedly and your growth and experience enrich Me.*"

28

DURING A STORM I WATCHED THE FURIOUS WAVES
POUNDING THE SHORE. THE ROCKS REMAINED FIRM
AND SOLID. ON A SUNNY DAY I WATCHED
THE PEACEFUL SEA GENTLY CARESS THE SHORE.
THE ROCKS REMAINED FIRM AND SOLID.

I heard the Voice say…

*"Whatever your emotions, your rages, your
frustrations or your joys, I am firm and solid in
My love for you."*

DURING MY JOURNEY I LOOKED OUT OF THE WINDOW AND SAW TREES OF EVERY SIZE AND SHAPE AND COLOUR. EACH WAS SPECIAL IN ITS OWN UNIQUE WAY. I LOVED THEM ALL. AND THERE WERE FLOWERS OF MANY VARIETIES AND HUES. EACH WAS BEAUTIFUL IN ITS OWN WAY. I LOVED THEM ALL. ON THE STATION THERE WERE PEOPLE OF EVERY NATIONALITY, SIZE, SHAPE AND COLOUR.

I heard the Voice say...

"Each of you is beautiful in your own special and unique way. I love you all."

As I LOOKED OUT OF THE AEROPLANE WINDOW
I COULD SEE A PATCHWORK OF FIELDS BELOW. THERE
WERE DARK PATCHES DOTTED HERE AND THERE.
FROM MY HIGH PERSPECTIVE I COULD SEE THAT
THESE WERE THE SHADOWS OF CLOUDS FLOATING
BETWEEN THE SUN AND THE EARTH.

I heard the Voice say…

"There is only shadow in your life where you block My Light. Like the clouds these troubles disperse and like the sun My Light is there for ever."

31

I WANTED TO DO HEALING AND SPIRITUAL WORK BUT
I THOUGHT I WOULD NOT BE ABLE TO EARN ENOUGH
MONEY TO LIVE. SO I HELD ONTO MY OLD JOB WHICH
WAS BORING AND FRUSTRATING.

I heard the Voice say…

*"When you worry about material things it is wasted
energy. When you work for Me I will meet your
material needs. Let go and trust."*

I WAS LAZY AND MY BODY FELT RIGIDLY STIFF
AND INFLEXIBLE.

I heard the Voice say...

"*Look after your body. Keep your joints flexible and free so My energy can flow through you. When your body is flowing you can be used as a channel for healing.*"

33

I SAW A SUIT OF ARMOUR AND IMAGINED A MAN INSIDE IT. HOW COULD HE CUDDLE HIS CHILDREN IN ARMOUR? HOW COULD HE MAKE LOVE TO HIS WIFE?.

I heard the Voice say…

"When you put up your emotional defences you are like the man in armour. Take it off now and open yourself to love and be loved."

34

THE BIRD IMPRISONED IN THE CAGE FLAPPED TO GET FREE. WHEN IT ESCAPED IT NEVER RETURNED. THE BIRDS WHICH WERE FREE TO COME OR GO CAME BACK TO MY GARDEN BECAUSE THEY LOVED ME AND WANTED TO BE WITH ME.

I heard the Voice say...

"*So it is with people. Release all your attachments. Let others be free and those who love you will always come back to you because they want to.*"

35

THE WOMAN LOVED HER CHILDREN AND WANTED THEM TO STAY CLOSE BUT THEY WANTED TO TRAVEL AND LIVE ABROAD. SHE FELT SAD AND ALONE.

I heard the Voice say...

"*Your children are entrusted to you. You are privileged to have the responsibility of a soul in your care. But they are only on loan to you. You must be prepared to let them go.*"

36

Out in the fields and woods I feel relaxed and happy. My worries and cares dissolve and seem unimportant. I wondered why this is always so.

I hearts the Voice say.

"*Green is the colour of the heart. When you are troubled and seek peace go into the green of nature. I am everywhere – but there you can find Me more easily.*"

37

IT WAS WARM AND COMFORTABLE IN THE HOUSE.
WE HAD EATEN WELL AND LAUGHED A GREAT DEAL.
OUTSIDE IT WAS COLD AND WINDY. A BEGGAR
KNOCKED ON MY DOOR AND I TURNED HIM AWAY.

I heard the Voice say...

"*When you reject a soul in need you reject Me for
I am in everyone. No one comes into your life but that
I send him. I sent this beggar to you that you may learn
to open your heart.*"

38

M FRIEND HAD DIED AND I MISSED HER SORELY.
I DREAMT THAT SHE CAME TO ME AND WE WERE
HAPPY TOGETHER.

I heard the Voice say...

"*You are a spirit whether in a body or out of it. Love can never be taken away. Your friend came to show you this. You cannot experience her physical presence but her love is with you.*"

39

I WATCHED A GROUP OF SMALL CHILDREN LAUGHING WITH PURE JOY AND I FOUND MYSELF SMILING.

I heard the Voice say…

"*A happy person is a whole and holy person. This is why laughter is My favourite music. It has a vibration of pure joy which sends beautiful colours out into the Universe and lights up the lives of others.*"

40

THE MAN WHISTLED TO HIS DOG. IN THE FAR DISTANCE THE DOG PRICKED UP HIS EARS AND LOOKED AROUND AS IF TO DETERMINE WHERE THE CALL CAME FROM. THE MAN WHISTLED AGAIN. THIS TIME THE DOG MOVED TOWARDS HIM, SLOWLY AT FIRST, AS IF UNCERTAIN OF THE DIRECTION. THEN AS THE CALL REACHED HIM CLEARLY, HE RACED STRAIGHT TO HIS MASTER.

I heard the Voice say...

"You are hesitant and unsure when first you hear My call. As you become attuned to Me, you hear My guidance more clearly. Listen intently and come on a direct path to Me."

41

I FELT MY HANDS HOT AND PULSATING. I WANTED TO USE THE ENERGY FOR HEALING BUT WAS AFRAID TO TRY. "WHAT IF IT DOESN'T WORK?" I THOUGHT.

I heard the Voice say...

"When you lay hands on another with love in your heart, a healing takes place. It may not manifest in the physical but the wisdom of the soul will use the energy where it is most needed. Always follow your impulse to heal and do it with love."

42

I LOOKED AT THE VAST, BLACK VELVET SKY SPANGLED WITH STARS. I FELT SMALL AND INSIGNIFICANT YET I FELT A PART OF SOMETHING IMPORTANT. WHAT WAS MY ROLE IN THIS GREAT UNIVERSE, I WONDERED?.

I heard the Voice say...

"*Every creature, plant or stone is important to Me. When you become aware of Me, you love and care for all around you, knowing in this way you serve Me. Your role is to love and be a teacher of love.*"

43

I LOOKED BEHIND EVERY TREE AND STONE FOR MY LIFE PURPOSE. "WHAT IS MY PURPOSE?" I CRIED OUT.

I heard the Voice say...

"*When you raise your consciousness and attune to Me, I will guide you. Stop all seeking and searching. As you rest and relax I will drop the thoughts you need into your mind. Your task is to listen and to act on My promptings. Then, with joy, you will discover your purpose.*"

44

How can I serve You better?" I cried.

I heard the Voice say...

"*Open yourself to Me. Cleanse and purify your vibrations. To do this go into nature or walk by running water to do this. Breathe deeply at all times. Every day read some inspirational work and focus on love and joy and the beautiful qualities of My Universe. Then you can raise your consciousness and attune to Me, and you become a pure channel for My work.*"

TWO ELDERLY SISTERS SAT SIDE BY SIDE ON A
BENCH. ONE LOOKED TIRED AND LINED. SHE CREAKED
WITH OLD AGE. THE OTHER, EQUALLY OLD, LOOKED
GLOWING AND HAPPY AND SPRIGHTLY. "HOW COULD
THIS BE SO?" I WONDERED.

I heard the Voice say...

*"The happy, glowing, sprightly sister works for Me.
She is a channel for my work and as My pure energy
flows through her, it keeps her young and beautiful. When
you become a channel for Me, you glow with My love."*

I WATCHED THE RIVER JOIN THE SEA. I WATCHED
THE TIDE FLOW IN OVER THE ROCKS UNTIL EACH
LITTLE ROCK POOL BECAME PART OF THE OCEAN
AGAIN. I WATCHED GREAT DROPS OF RAIN FROM THE
CLOUDS OVERHEAD FALL INTO THE SEA.

I heard the Voice say...

"*I am like the sea. You are all part of Me and you
all return in your own way to become one with Me.*"

47

EVERYWHERE WE DROVE THERE WERE TRAFFIC JAMS. WE MOVED FROM ONE HOLD UP TO ANOTHER AND I SEETHED WITH IMPATIENCE. I WAS SURE WE WOULD BE TOO LATE TO GET A TABLE AT OUR DESTINATION. SUDDENLY THE HOLD-UPS CLEARED AND WE WERE FREE. AS WE ARRIVED AT THE RESTAURANT, A WHOLE PARTY OF PEOPLE LEFT AND WE HAD A PERFECT TABLE.

I heard the Voice say...

"*Trust Me. My timing is always perfect and I teach you lessons on the way.*"

48

FEELING ANGRY, I WAS DRAWN TO WATCH THE LION IN ITS CAGE. IT PACED TO AND FRO RESENTING THE RESTRICTIONS.

I heard the Voice say...

"*Only your consciousness cages you. In truth you are free. And when you free yourself of limitation by opening to Me you will never feel caged again. And when humankind frees its own caged consciousness, it will never cage an animal again.*"

I LOOKED AT THE SICK WOMAN AND KNEW THAT HER
FEAR OF HER HUSBAND LEAVING KEPT HER ILL.
SHE KNEW HE WOULD NEVER LEAVE A SICK WIFE.
"HOW DOES HER ILLNESS SERVE YOU?" I ASKED.

I heard the Voice say...

"*Her fear of aloneness and separation keeps her ill.
When she remembers Me she will know there is no
separation. Then the illness will have served its purpose.
Fear always serves Love.*"

50

THE SEVERELY HANDICAPPED MAN SLUMPED IN HIS WHEELCHAIR. HE COULD DO NOTHING FOR HIMSELF. "WHAT USE IS HE?" I ASKED.

I heard the Voice say...

"He serves Me with his heart and soul. He is a mighty spiritual warrior, living a life of total submission. Never judge another soul. He may have undertaken a very difficult task to test his courage."

51

I AMBLED ACROSS THE MEADOW ON THE WAY HOME. I FELT IRRITATED WHEN I FELT THE FIRST SPLASH OF RAIN. THEN IT RAINED HARDER AND I RAN ALL THE WAY HOME.

I heard the Voice say...

"The rain, which you considered irritating and negative served you. It caused you to reach home more quickly. Seemingly irritating and negative happenings all serve a purpose. They all hasten you on your journey Home to Me."

52

THE WOMAN HELD A SKEIN OF WOOL ON HER LAP.
THE WOOL SEEMED SO TANGLED AND KNOTTED,
I THOUGHT IT WOULD BE IMPOSSIBLE TO UNRAVEL.
BUT SHE SAT THERE PATIENTLY TEASING OUT THE
KNOTS AND CAREFULLY SORTING OUT THE TANGLES
UNTIL SHE HELD AN ORDERED BALL OF WOOL IN HER
HANDS READY TO USE.

I heard the Voice say...

"*You too can un-knot your beliefs and straighten out
your thoughts. Then you will be ready for Me to use.*"

53

I WAS SO ANGRY AT WHAT I SAW THAT I DID WHAT
I COULD TO HELP THOSE UNJUSTLY TREATED.
THEN I WROTE LETTERS ABOUT IT TO EVERYONE
I COULD THINK OF TO DRAW THE INJUSTICE TO
PUBLIC AWARENESS.

I heard the Voice say...

*"Blessed is your anger for it is the fire which has
driven you to right the wrongs you see. Anger rightly used
is My Fire."*

54

I PASSED A GARDEN WHERE THE LAWN WAS OVERGROWN AND THE FLOWERBEDS CHOKED WITH WEEDS. IT WAS AN UNATTRACTIVE MESS. SOME WEEKS LATER WHEN I PASSED THE SAME GARDEN THE LAWN HAD BEEN CUT AND ITS EDGES TRIMMED. THE FLOWER BEDS HAD BEEN WEEDED AND NOW BLOOMED WITH COLOUR. IT WAS BEAUTIFUL AND I LINGERED TO ENJOY IT.

I heard the Voice say…

"When you weed out the negative beliefs which choke your consciousness, you bloom and become beautified Then people want to be with you to enjoy your beauty."

55

THE FARMER PREPARED HIS LAND WITH MUCH EFFORT AND CARE. THEN HE SOWED TOP QUALITY SEED. THROUGHOUT THE SEASON HE TENDED HIS GROWING CROPS TO THE VERY BEST OF HIS ABILITY. IN THE AUTUMN HE HAD A BUMPER HARVEST.

I heard the Voice say...

"*Do your best. Put all the effort you can into what you do. You will be well pleased with the result.*"

THE WOMAN HAD A VISION – SOME WOULD CALL IT A DREAM – WHICH CHANGED HER LIFE. MANY SAID TO HER. "WHY YOU? WHY CAN'T I BE SO LUCKY?" I PONDERED ON THIS.

I heard the Voice say…

"*I try to get through to everyone, however closed, at least once. Most people doubt their vision and within the hour or week or year, they let it fade. That woman never doubted hers and she held onto it until it filled her consciousness and changed her life.*"

57

THE BURGLAR ENJOYED HIS ILL–GOTTEN GAINS. THE FRAUDULENT BUSINESSMAN LIVED IN LUXURY ABROAD. THE CHEAT GOT AWAY WITH HIS DECEPTION. "HOW COULD THIS BE?" I WONDERED.

I heard the Voice say...

"*Where you can do something to right injustice, do it. Where you cannot, do not waste energy on worry or thoughts of vengeance. Leave it to Me for the working out of all things under Spiritual Law is exact. It may take lifetimes but all injustice is righted in the end.*"

58

I WATCHED A MAN ON CRUTCHES. DOCTORS TOLD HIM HE WOULD NEVER WALK UNAIDED BUT HE WAS DETERMINED. HE EXERCISED HOUR AFTER HOUR TO STRENGTHEN HIS MUSCLES UNTIL HE NEEDED ONLY A STICK TO SUPPORT HIM. THEN THE DAY CAME WHEN HE COULD THROW THAT TOO AWAY. HE WALKED FREELY ON STRONG LEGS.

I heard the Voice say...

"You too must strengthen yourself in every area until you can throw away your emotional crutches."

THE LITTLE FLOWER WAS BEATEN BY THE BITTER
SLEET. AT NIGHT IT WAS FROZEN BY THE ICY FROST.
IT SHRIVELLED AND NEARLY DIED. IT WAS ONLY WHEN
THE SUN WARMED IT AND THE GENTLE RAIN
NOURISHED IT THAT IT STARTED TO GROW AGAIN.

I heard the Voice say…

*"And you are like that delicate flower. Your self
critical, harsh thoughts are the icy frost that stultify you.
Each happy and nourishing thought that you have
encourages you to grow."*

I LAY AND BASKED IN THE GOLDEN RAYS OF THE
SUN. I FELL ASLEEP IN ITS WARMTH AND WHEN
I WOKE THE SUN HAD DISAPPEARED BEHIND A CLOUD.
I SHIVERED AND WONDERED IF THE SUN WOULD EVER
SHINE AGAIN. IT DID.

I heard the Voice say...

*"There are times when your dark thoughts are like
clouds blocking you from My warmth and light. Know
always that I am waiting to shine on you again."*

THE IVY CLUNG TO THE LOG SMOTHERING IT
COMPLETELY. THE LOG LOOKED SECURE BUT WHEN
I STEPPED ONTO IT, IT COLLAPSED UNDER ME.
I SAW IT WAS HOLLOW AND EMPTY.

I heard the Voice say...

"*You are hollow and empty when you cling to one
another through fear and need. Become strong
and independent. I will support you and fulfil
all your needs.*"

In the cool of the early morning I saw a tightly closed bud. As the sun shone the bud began to open. Its petals gradually unfurled and spread wider and wider until the flower was completely open for all to enjoy its fragrance.

I heard the Voice say...

"And as you respond to Me your heart gently expands. When you are fully in My Light your heart opens wide. Then you radiate My Essence for all to enjoy."

63

I SAT ON THE CLIFF TOP AND GAZED AT THE EMPTY SEA. NO BOAT WAS TO BE SEEN. NOTHING STIRRED. YET I KNEW THAT UNDER ITS SURFACE THERE WAS A HIDDEN WORLD OF ACTIVITY TAKING PLACE. THERE WAS UNIMAGINABLE BEAUTY AND TREASURE TO BE FOUND.

I heard the Voice say...

"*When you feel empty, dive into the depths of your being. You will find an inner world to explore. And in your inner world you will find Me.*"

As I SURVEYED THE BEAUTIFUL VIEW THE FIRE
CHARRED HILLSIDE STOOD OUT LIKE AN UGLY SCAR.
IT REMINDED ME OF SOMETHING I HAD DONE YEARS
BEFORE WHEN T FELT THAT MY GUILT STOOD OUT
LIKE A SCAR FOR ALL TO SEE. YEARS LATER THAT
HILL WAS GREEN. THERE WAS NO SCAR. I SAW ONLY
A BEAUTIFUL PANORAMA.

I heard the Voice say…

*"Forgive yourself and the green mantle of love will
transform your guilt. Then when others see you, they will
see only a Being of Love."*

I KNEW A WISE MAN WHO ALWAYS TRIED TO HELP OTHERS. HE ALWAYS LOOKED FOR THE POSITIVE IN EVERYTHING.

I heard the Voice say...

"When you focus on beauty and you work for the good of mankind, you are a Light Worker. Then you leave golden footsteps wherever you walk."

THE COUPLE WERE PORING OVER A JIGSAW PUZZLE. THEY TRIED TO MATCH SHAPES AND COLOURS AS THEY SLOTTED PIECES TOGETHER – THEY STRUGGLED TO UNDERSTAND WHERE CERTAIN PIECES FITTED. THEN THE JIGSAW WAS COMPLETE AND THEY COULD SEE THE WHOLE PICTURE. ALL WAS MADE CLEAR.

I heard the Voice say...

"*Your life is like a jigsaw. You struggle and worry about things because you do not see the complete picture. Do your best and know that I see everything and all is working out perfectly.*"

67

THE CHILD WOULD NOT PARTICIPATE THAT DAY.
SHE LOOKED MISERABLE AND SORRY FOR HERSELF.
SHE SAID SHE FELT SAD. THE TEACHER SUGGESTED
SHE WOULD FEEL BETTER IF SHE JOINED IN INSTEAD
OF SITTING APART. EVENTUALLY THE CHILD DECIDED
TO JOIN IN THE GAME AND SOON HER SADNESS
DISSOLVED AND SHE WAS HAPPY AND LAUGHING.

I heard the Voice say...

*"When you participate fully in the game of life
My Joy flows through you. That is your way
to happiness."*

68

I TURNED THE KNOB OF MY RADIO AND PICKED UP A VARIETY OF STATIONS BUT NOTHING WAS WORTH LISTENING TO. I CONTINUED TO TUNE INTO DIFFERENT WAVELENGTHS UNTIL I HEARD LOUD AND CLEAR THE PROGRAMME I WANTED TO HEAR.

I heard the Voice say…

"I am constantly broadcasting. Use meditation to tune in until you find My wavelength. Then you will hear the clear note of My Truth."

As I WAS DRIVING DOWN THE ROAD THE TRAFFIC AHEAD STARTED TO BUNCH UP. DRIVERS HAD SLOWED DOWN TO LOOK AT AN ACCIDENT. ONE DRIVER HAD SWERVED AND NEARLY HIT ANOTHER IN HIS CURIOSITY TO SEE.

I heard the Voice say...

"Unless you can help directly, do not be deflected by or give energy to another's misfortune. Keep your eyes on your path ahead. Focus your attention on Me."

70

On one side of the river the bank was dark and shadowed by overhanging trees. On the other it was light and open. I looked straight ahead and saw only the sun shining on the water.

I heard the Voice say...

"When you see the good and bad in others you see their duality. Look beyond to their God Selves and then you will find oneness. There you will find Me."

I OFTEN WALKED THIS WOODLAND PATH. IN SOME PLACES I HAD TO WADE THROUGH PUDDLES AND MUD. ONE DAY I NOTICED A SECOND PATH HIGHER UP THE HILLSIDE. IT WAS DRY AND PLEASANT, RUNNING PARALLEL TO THE MUDDY ONE.

I heard the Voice say…

"If your way in life seems muddy and slippery, look up. Raise your consciousness and seek a Higher Path to Me."

A STRING OF COLOURED LIGHTS GLOWED IN THE DARKNESS. THE BULBS WERE DIFFERENT COLOURS, SHAPES AND SIZES. A FEW HIGH WATTAGE BULBS WERE BRIGHTER THAN THE REST. YET THE SAME CURRENT LIT THEM ALL.

I heard the Voice say...

"Some of you shine with more God force than others."

THE MAN WAS SO DEPRESSED I COULD SENSE
THE DARKNESS AROUND HIM. NO ONE COULD
LIGHTEN HIS MISERY.

I heard the Voice say...

"*When you lose your connection with Me you are in the dark. I am the current that lights you up. Plug directly into Me and I will light up your life.*"

THE HOUSE WAS SHORED UP WITH SCAFFOLDING WHILE THE BUILDING WORK TOOK PLACE. WHEN IT WAS COMPLETED THE BUILDERS TOOK THE SCAFFOLDING AWAY.

I heard the Voice say…

"While you are working on yourself I am your scaffolding. I hold you up. Only when you are reinforced with My wisdom do I let you stand alone."

75

I WATCHED A GROUP OF CHILDREN PLAYING.
ONE WANTED TO BE 'IT'. WHEN SHE DIDN'T GET HER
WAY SHE BECAME CROSS AND SULKY. FOR THE REST
OF THE DAY SHE SAT APART FROM THE REST
REFUSING TO JOIN IN. A FEW DAYS LATER SHE HAD
LET GO OF HER DESIRE TO BE 'IT' AND WAS PLAYING
HAPPILY WITH THE OTHERS. I SMILED AS
I WATCHED HER.

I heard the Voice say…

"Let go of your attachment to what you want and throw yourself into all that life offers you. Then I smile as I watch you."

76

WIND AND RAIN LASHED THE POOL. IN THE MUD
THROWN UP BY THE TURBULENCE I COULD SEE
NOTHING. WHEN THE WEATHER CALMED THE POOL
BECAME STILL. ALL WAS CRYSTAL CLEAR.

I heard the Voice say...

"*Your emotions are like the weather. When they
are turbulent you cannot see anything clearly.
When they are still everything is clear. So keep
yourself calm and still at all times. In the clarity you
will find Me.*"

77

I WALKED THROUGH THE GARDENS. THE BLOOMS WERE VIBRANT IN THE SUNSHINE. THE WATER OF THE FOUNTAIN SHIMMERED IN THE LIGHT. I REVELLED IN THE BEAUTY. THEN I WALKED UNDER THE DARK TREES WHERE IT WAS COLD AND SHADOWY. IT SMELT DANK AND I SHIVERED.

I heard the Voice say…

"*Everything is part of Me – the Shadow and the Light. Accept all things. All is Divine.*"

78

A MOTHER HAD SEVERAL CHILDREN ALL WITH DIFFERENT GIFTS AND ABILITIES. SHE LOVED THEM ALL BUT THE ONE WHO GAVE HER GREATEST PLEASURE WAS THE ONE WHO REALLY ENJOYED HERSELF. AT THE SAME TIME SHE DID HER BEST.

I heard the Voice say…

"*You all have different gifts and abilities. I love you all but I rejoice with those of you who use your talents to the full and enjoy doing so. Laugh often and do your best.*"

WHEN THE CHILDREN HAD BEEN TAUGHT THEIR LESSONS THEIR TEACHER TESTED THEM TO SEE HOW WELL THEY HAD LEARNT. WHEN THEY WERE READY THEY COULD MOVE UP TO A HIGHER CLASS.

I heard the Voice say...

"Life on Earth is My school, so rejoice when you have a testing time. Each time you pass one of My tests you are ready to move nearer to Me."

Thiere were so many paths up the mountain that I asked which one to take. I was told that each was challenging in its way but I could reach the summit by any of them.

I heard the Voice say…

"All religions are a Path to Me. They represent different challenges on the way. So respect the Paths chosen by others. Respect every religion but listen only to Me."

I HEARD BIRDS CAWING IN RAUCOUS NOTES.
OTHERS SANG BEAUTIFUL SONGS. WHY WERE THEY
SO DIFFERENT I WONDERED?.

I heard the Voice say…

"*Each creature expresses according to its nature. You too express according to your nature but you can choose how you express. Choose sweet words, gently spoken and I will listen with delight.*"

THE NOTES OF THE PIANO WERE DISCORDANT AND OUT OF TUNE. AS A RESULT THE WHOLE ORCHESTRA WAS OFF KEY. WHEN THE PIANO WAS RETUNED EVERYONE PLAYED IN HARMONY.

I heard the Voice say...

"*When you feel discordant and off key everything goes wrong in your life. Centre yourself. Get back in tune and everything in your life will be in harmony again.*"

THE CLOTH WAS WHITE UNTIL IT WAS IMPRINTED WITH A PATTERN. TO MAKE IT WHITE AGAIN I HAD TO MAKE A DETERMINED EFFORT TO WASH AND SCRUB AND BOIL IT.

I heard the Voice say...

"Your impure thoughts are deeply ingrained patterns which need to be cleansed and purified. Make a determined effort and you will become pure again."

84

I WATCHED PEOPLE WADING MISERABLY THROUGH
THE MUD COMPLAINING AS THEY WENT.

I heard the Voice say...

"When you wallow in self pity you wade through the mud of selfishness. Transcend your emotions and you will be on the clean, dry path to Me."

85

On the plains there were people everywhere warming themselves by fires. Some fires were small. Others were so huge that they warmed many people.

I heard the Voice say…

"Within each of you is a Divine flame. Fan your flame with right thinking so that it grows into a huge flame which warms many people around you."

86

I THOUGHT THE FLAME HAD GONE OUT BUT THE MAN SAW A SPARK AND PATIENTLY FANNED IT UNTIL IT FLICKERED TO LIFE. HE CONTINUED TO FAN IT AND FEED IT UNTIL IT BECAME A HUGE FIRE.

I heard the Voice say...

"*There is a spark of Me in everyone however wicked they appear to be. Fan this spark in yourself and others until God-consciousness is a huge flame.*"

87

THE YOUNG MAN SLIPPED THE RING ONTO HIS
BRIDE'S FINGER. HER EYES SHONE WITH JOY AND
DELIGHT AND HE WANTED TO GIVE HER THE WORLD.

I heard the Voice say...

*"When you receive my token of Love with joy
and delight I want to bestow more and more on you.
So open yourselves to receive with joy and I will create
My World in you."*

88

THE WOMAN WATCHED HERSELF IN THE MIRROR WHILE SHE COMBED HER HAIR. AS HER HAIR BECAME NEAT AND TIDY THE REFLECTION CHANGED.

I heard the Voice say…

"*You cannot change another person. They are reflections of aspects of you. Change yourself and the reflection will change. Change yourself and you will transform all your relationships.*"

At FIRST I THOUGHT THE MAN WOULD NEVER MASTER THE WILD HORSE. BUT WITH FIRMNESS AND DISCIPLINE HE TAMED THE ANIMAL. THEN IT WAS A JOY TO WATCH THEM WORK TOGETHER WITH MUTUAL LOVE AND RESPECT.

I heard the Voice say...

"Your emotions are like that wild horse. Master them with firmness and discipline. Then you will be respected and loved by all and you will be ready to work more closely with Me."

90

I FELT UPSET AFTER WATCHING AN UNPLEASANT FILM ABOUT VIOLENCE AND CORRUPTION.

I heard the Voice say…

"What you say and what you hear influence you unconsciously. Sing or chant hymns of glory to Me. Listen to inspirational words. This influences you for your Higher Good without you even realising it."

EVERY DAY THE MOTHER PRAYED FOR HER CHILD.
WHEN HER CHILD WAS IN DANGER HE WAS SAVED,
FOR THE MOTHER'S PRAYER PUT A BUFFER OF
PROTECTION ROUND HIM.

I heard the Voice say...

"*Prayer is a divine energy which protects and heals.
Always remember its power.*"

THE MAN LASHED THE DOG TO BEAT IT INTO SUBMISSION. HE THOUGHT HE COULD MASTER IT BY BREAKING ITS SPIRIT. THE DOG SUBMITTED WITH HATRED AND WITH A DESIRE FOR REVENGE IN ITS HEART.

I heard the Voice say...

"Never try to control another by force. That is not mastery. Rather seek to gain his respect by self discipline and non violence. Then you will gain true mastery. Love is more powerful than any beating. I conquer your hearts with love."

93

THE SKY WAS DARK AND HEAVY AFTER THE RAIN.
I FELT SAD AND DEPRESSED. THEN I LOOKED UP AND
SAW THE RAINBOW. IT WAS LIKE A SIGN – A PROMISE
OF HOPE ACROSS THE SKY.

I heard the Voice say...

*"Whenever you are sad or depressed look up and I
will give you a sign of hope. I am always there waiting
for you to look up."*

THE WOMAN WAS WRACKED WITH PAIN. "WHY?"
I ASKED.

I heard the Voice say…

"*You have pain when you lose your connection with Me. Pain makes you look within for answers. It causes you to seek to connect with Me at your centre. If you would only keep looking within and connecting with Me you would never need the reminder of pain.*"

95

THE MAN TOLD HIS DOGS TO STAY TO HEEL. THEY
COULD ONLY SEE THE COUNTRY LANE AND HATED
BEING HELD BACK. THEIR OWNER KNEW THAT THERE
WAS A ROAD AHEAD WHICH THEY MUST SAFELY CROSS
BEFORE THEY COULD RUN FREE.

I heard the Voice say...

"*When I hold you back it is always for your greater good. Trust Me. Be patient and I will give you opportunities when the time is right.*"

96

ONE MAN SIGNED UP FOR AN EASY COURSE.
HE WAS SOON BORED. ANOTHER SIGNED UP FOR
A DIFFICULT COURSE. HE STRUGGLED TO LEARN
BUT IT EXTENDED HIM ENORMOUSLY.

I heard the Voice say...

"*Your current situation is the course you have signed up for in the school of Earth. Never complain. You chose that lesson. Understand why you are in your present circumstances. Learn quickly from your situation. Master the lesson and move on.*"

97

IF YOU PUT A LOW VOLUME OF ENERGY THROUGH A LIGHT BULB YOU WILL GET A FAINT RED GLOW. AS YOU INCREASE THE ENERGY THE BULB EMITS MORE COLOURS – THROUGH ORANGE, YELLOW, GREEN, BLUE, INDIGO AND VIOLET – UNTIL IT RADIATES THE COMPLETE SPECTRUM.

I heard the Voice say…

"When you give all your energy to Me you radiate the full spectrum. Then you are White Light. And you are a beacon of light on Earth."

SOME OF THE PEOPLE AT WORK WERE CONSTANTLY
ANGRY AND COMPLAINING AND IT FELT UNPLEASANT.
I DID NOT KNOW WHAT TO DO ABOUT IT.

I heard the Voice say…

"*You are a magnet and like a magnet you attract
people and situations to your vibration. If you do not like
what you attract raise your vibration to a higher level.
Then you will magnetise more harmonious conditions
and people into your life.*"

I RENTED A COTTAGE BY THE SEA AND FROM
THE WINDOW I COULD SEE THE LIGHTHOUSE BEACON
CONSTANTLY FLASHING TO GUIDE THE SHIPS.
ON FOGGY NIGHTS I COULD NOT SEE THE LIGHT
BUT I COULD HEAR THE FOG HORN KEEPING
THE SHIPS SAFE.

I heard the Voice say…

*"My Light shines steadfastly to direct you.
When you cannot see My Light, listen and you will
hear my promptings. I will guide you and keep
you safe."*

100

THE BOY THREW STICKS UP INTO THE PLUM TREE TO KNOCK DOWN THE PLUMS. HE DAMAGED THE TREE AND THE PLUMS WERE TOO UNRIPE TO ENJOY. THE MAN WAITED UNTIL THE TIME WAS RIGHT AND THEN THE PLUMS DROPPED, RIPE AND READY TO EAT, INTO HIS HANDS.

I heard the Voice say...

"*When you are impatient and greedy your efforts will not be rewarded. Relax and be patient. I know when the time is right and then everything will come to you easily in a perfect way.*"

101

I WATCHED THE HOT ORANGE FLAMES BURN ALL THE WOOD AWAY UNTIL THERE WAS ONLY FINE ASH LEFT.

I heard the Voice say…

"*Life's experiences are the flames which burn away your ego until there is only spirit left. Then you are purified and ready to return to Me.*"

102

I WATCHED THE MAN POKING THE BONFIRE WITH A STICK. IMMEDIATELY SHOWERS OF SPARKS WERE RELEASED AND FLEW ALL OVER THE PLACE, LIGHTING UP THE DARK NIGHT.

I heard the Voice say...

"Sometimes I poke you so that you may release the sparks of Divinity within you. If I did not poke you, you would not know you had the sparks of faith, strength, caring, patience and a million other qualities within you. These light up your darkness."

103

I WATCHED THE FOOTBALLER KICKING THE BALL. I NOTICED THAT WHEN HE PASSED IT TO ANOTHER PLAYER HE IMMEDIATELY RAN TO HIS NEXT POSITION WITHOUT CHECKING IT HAD BEEN RECEIVED. THAT WAY HE WAS IN THE RIGHT PLACE FOR THE NEXT PASS AND WAS ON THE WINNING SIDE.

I heard the Voice say...

"When you hand your burdens to Me, assume I have taken them and position yourself for the next step in your life trusting I have received your burden from you. That is how to play the game of life and win."

104

THE LADY WORKED HARD AND WAS QUIET AND GOOD
BUT WAS BORED WITH HER JOB. ONE DAY SHE WAS
INVITED TO DO A DIFFERENT JOB. SUDDENLY SHE
FELT ALIVE, INTERESTED, ENTHUSIASTIC AND HAPPY,
BUT SHE FELT GUILTY THAT SHE WAS ENJOYING
HERSELF SO MUCH. SURELY THAT WAS NOT RIGHT?

I heard the Voice say…

*"When you work with an open heart you are
working for Me. Aliveness, enthusiasm and happiness
are Divine energies. Be joyful!"*

105

I NOTICED THE PLANT STRUGGLING IN POOR SOIL IN ADVERSE CONDITIONS AND IT LOOKED FEEBLE AND WILTING. THE GARDENER MOVED IT TO RICH SOIL IN A SHELTERED, SUNNY POSITION. HE TENDED IT CAREFULLY AND THE PLANT QUICKLY GREW AND BLOSSOMED.

I heard the Voice say...

"*You are like that plant. If you are in an adverse job, relationship or conditions you wilt and decline. So take care of your needs and move to a place where you can blossom in My Light.*"

106

THE BONFIRE FLARED BRIGHTLY IN THE DARKNESS.
WHEN I PUT A BIG LOG ON IT, IT SEEMED TO DAMP IT
DOWN AND ALMOST PUT IT OUT, BUT EVENTUALLY
THE WHOLE FIRE BURNED BRIGHTER THAN EVER.

I heard the Voice say...

*"Sometimes I put great responsibility on you and
you may feel crushed for a while. But as you accept
and learn from the responsibility you become stronger
and, therefore, a brighter light."*

107

THE SEED LAY IN THE COLD GROUND FOR A LONG
TIME BEFORE A GREEN SHOOT APPEARED.
MUCH LATER A BUD FORMED WITH THE PROMISE
OF A PERFECT FLOWER.

I heard the Voice say...

*"During periods of uncertainty remain quiet
and dormant. This is the time to wait for clarity.
At the right time the perfect idea will germinate
and eventually flower."*

108

ONE RIVER GUSHED DOWN THE GORGE IN A
WHITE RACING TORRENT. IT WAS EXCITING TO WATCH.
ANOTHER MEANDERED LAZILY THROUGH GREEN
MEADOWS. IT WAS PEACEFUL TO SEE.

I heard the Voice say...

"*Some of you rush and race through life.
Others gently flow. Whether you choose to live a life
of excitement or one of peace, you all return to Me.*"

109

THE RICH MAN PUBLICLY GAVE MONEY TO CHARITY. EVERYONE SAID HOW GENEROUS HE WAS AND HE BASKED IN THEIR PRAISE. ANOTHER QUIETLY DONATED WHAT HE COULD AND NO ONE KNEW.

I heard the Voice say...

"*When you give to another with a desire for honour it is a selfish action. I give you no reward. When you give without desire for personal thanks, you bask in My rewards. Always examine your motives.*"

110

ON THE TREES THAT HAD GROWN WILD, THE FRUIT WAS FULL OF MAGGOTS. WHERE THE TREES WERE CAREFULLY CULTIVATED THE FRUIT WAS SOUND AND GOOD.

I heard the Voice say...

"*Where you are selfish, conceited and addicted to sensuous enjoyment, you are like the tree that has grown wild. Your life is rotten. Discipline, self awareness and good intention produce good stock and the fruits of your life will be sound.*"

THE VAST RESERVOIR WAS FILLED WITH WATER.
IT SERVED MANY TOWNS AND VILLAGES. I REALISED
THAT IF THE CONTAINING WALLS COLLAPSED THE
WATER COULD DO IMMENSE DAMAGE TO THOSE SAME
TOWNS AND VILLAGES

I heard the Voice say…

"*You are a vast reservoir of My Power.
You can use it to serve others or hurt them. So be careful.
Direct your life force for good.*"

I WATCHED THE PLAY AND FOUND IT VERY INTERESTING. THEN I JOINED THE CAST AND UNDERSTOOD THE PLANNING AND PREPARATION THAT WENT INTO THE PRESENTATION. NOW I WAS FASCINATED AND SAW EVERYTHING FROM A WIDER PERSPECTIVE.

I heard the Voice say...

"*You are acting out the play of your life. What is happening now is based on much behind the scenes activity that has taken place over many years. Don't be an observer. Participate fully in life and become aware of the wider perspective.*"

113

As THE PRODUCER OF THE PLAY I NOTICED
SEVERAL THINGS WHICH COULD BE IMPROVED.
BEFORE THE NEXT DAY I SPOKE TO THE CAST AND
THEY REHEARSED THE CHANGES SO THAT THE NEXT
PERFORMANCE WAS BETTER.

I heard the Voice say...

" *You produce the play of your life. Observe it closely and if you need to make changes do it before the next day begins.*"

I SEARCHED AND SEARCHED FOR THE PATH.
I KEPT GOING THE WRONG WAY AND STRUGGLED
THROUGH BRAMBLES AND UNDERGROWTH. I WAS
DETERMINED TO FIND THE PATH AND AT LAST
I FOUND IT AND KNEW IT WAS THE RIGHT ONE.
"WHY DIDN'T YOU SHOW ME EARLIER?" I CRIED.

I heard the Voice say

"If I had led you straight to your path you would not have the strength you now have. I had to check you were committed to finding and walking your true path."

I WATCHED THE POTTER MAKE THE JUG, TESTING IT UNTIL IT WAS PERFECTLY FORMED. THEN HE FIRED IT SO THAT IT WAS STRONG AND WOULD CARRY WATER.

I heard the Voice say...

"*You must prepare yourself as a vessel for Me. I am the water. You are the vessel. I am the Power. You are the container.*"

As I sat in a reverie I saw a vision of my possible future. My heart sang with joy and wonder. As the day went on I thought sadly, "It was just an impossible dream".

I heard the Voice say...

"At moments like these I slip visions into your mind. Do not let your doubts and fears destroy these visions. Hold them and bring them about. Everything is possible for I will support you.".

TWO WILD TIGERS WERE CONFINED IN TINY CAGES. ONE BECAME DEJECTED AND DISPIRITED AND LAY MISERABLY IN ITS CAGE ALL DAY. THE OTHER WENT WILD, ROARING, RAGING AND CLAWING AT EVERYONE, BECOMING UNMANAGEABLE.

EVENTUALLY IT WAS RELEASED AGAIN INTO THE JUNGLE WHERE IT COULD BE NATURAL AND FREE.

I heard the Voice say...

"*If you cage up your emotions you may become depressed and lifeless like the first tiger or you may fear losing control so that they break free and harm you. Release yourself and be your natural self. Then you will have power and energy to do magnificent work for Me.*"

118

I SAT IN THE WOODS AND WATCHED THE SUN
SHINING THROUGH THE LIGHT GREEN LEAVES. THEY
LOOKED BEAUTIFUL, SO LUMINOUS AND
TRANSPARENT.

I heard the Voice say…

"*When you glow with My Light you become luminous, transparent and very beautiful to all who look at you. This is how I see you at all times.*"

119

THE ATHLETE WAS AIMING FOR A GOLD MEDAL. HE SPENT HIS TIME TRAINING SO THAT HE WOULD BE IN PEAK CONDITION. HE DENIED HIMSELF MANY PLEASURES, FOR EVERYTHING HE ATE OR SAID OR DID WAS FOCUSED ON ATTAINING HIS ULTIMATE GOAL. AND WHEN HE SUCCEEDED AND WORE THE GOLDEN MEDAL HE KNEW IT WAS WORTH IT.

I heard the Voice say...

"When you aim to ascend to My Kingdom you deny yourself many pleasures. Life is like an athlete's training. Everything you think, say, do or eat affects your chances of success. Keep your aim focused and when you come to Me you will know it was worth it."

120

Everyone was given a sheet of paper and invited to write about the future they saw for themselves. Some people wrote easily and fluently. Others hesitantly. One person did not write anything and eventually others filled in his paper for him.

I heard the Voice say...

"*Your life is like a blank sheet of paper. It is yours to write on. If you do not take the opportunity to write the story of your life, someone else will surely take over and write your life for you.*"

IT WAS ONE OF THE MOST CHALLENGING MOUNTAINS IN THE WORLD AND PEOPLE CAME FROM FAR AND WIDE TO CLIMB IT. SOME CLIMBED, CONQUERED AND LEFT AS HEROS. OTHERS BECAME LAZY, STAYED AND LIVED IN SHANTY TOWNS IN THE FOOTHILLS, FORGETTING THEIR AMBITION TO REACH THE TOP OF THE MOUNTAIN.

I heard the Voice say...

"Many accept the challenge to come to planet Earth and conquer its lessons. Some learn, ascend and leave as masters. Others stay, become lazy and forget what they are here to do. I remind you, all came to climb this most challenging spiritual mountain."

THE FRIENDS WERE CHUGGING ALONG THE RIVER
IN A BOAT. THEY WERE HAVING FUN AND PAYING NO
ATTENTION TO WHERE THEY WERE GOING. SUDDENLY
THE BOAT HIT A ROCK AND THEY ALL TUMBLED
INTO THE WATER.

I heard the Voice say...

"Look where you are going on the river of life. When you are unprepared for challenges, they hit you and you can get tumbled into turbulent emotions."

THE WOMAN PLANNED TO DO A TRIP BUT
EVERYTHING CONSPIRED TO STOP HER GOING. SHE
GRUMBLED AND CURSED AT FATE. A FEW MONTHS
LATER SHE ORGANISED A DIFFERENT TRIP, WHICH
EXCEEDED HER WILDEST DREAMS.

I heard the Voice say...

"*When something does not work out know that it is
not right for you at that time. I may have something
much better in store for you. Complaining and grumbling
may stop My greater plan from coming to fruition.*"

THE SOLDIER WAS SENT ON A MISSION INTO A DENSE FOREST. HE WAS TOLD TO MAKE DAILY RADIO CONTACT TO RECEIVE HELP AND INSTRUCTIONS. HOWEVER HE WAS TOO BUSY AND EVENTUALLY GOT HOPELESSLY LOST AND DISPIRITED. WHEN HE DID REMEMBER TO MAKE CONTACT HE HAD TO RETRACE HIS STEPS OVER DIFFICULT TERRAIN.

I heard the Voice say...

"*In your mission on Earth remember to make daily contact with Me through meditation and prayer so that I can guide and help you at all times. When you are too busy to do this you easily wander off your pathway and become lost. Then life appears frightening.*"

THE MISER SPENT ALL HIS TIME COUNTING HIS MONEY. WHEN HIS HOUSE BURNT DOWN HE LOST IT ALL. THE BUSINESS MAN SPENT ALL HIS ENERGY MAKING MONEY. THE BUSINESS COLLAPSED AND HE LOST IT ALL. THEY BOTH FELT WORTHLESS BECAUSE THEIR IDENTITY WAS BASED ON THEIR WEALTH.

I heard the Voice say...

"Material things can be taken away. When you spend your time and energy developing your gifts and talents, these are always with you. You will be valued for your wisdom and knowledge no matter what happens in your life."

126

THE MAN WORKED IN A FRENETIC PLACE, WENT TO RAUCOUS PARTIES AND HAD MANY LOUD, BOISTEROUS FRIENDS. HE CONSTANTLY COMPLAINED THAT HE COULD NOT FIND ANY PEACE.

I heard the Voice say…

"*If you wish to live in peace seek a peaceful work place. If you want serenity talk with serene people. If you seek harmony walk with harmonious people.*"

127

I WATCHED AS ALL THE SEEDS BLEW FROM THE PLANTS AND FLOATED IN THE AIR BEFORE SETTLING ONTO A TARMAC ROAD. I KNEW NONE OF THEM WOULD GERMINATE. IT SEEMED SUCH A WASTE.

I heard the Voice say...

"*You are my messengers on Earth. When you speak on My behalf be careful where you spread precious words of wisdom. Do not waste them on closed minds.*"

THE BOY WAS FRUSTRATED WHEN USING THE COMPUTER. IT REFUSED TO DO WHAT HE WANTED IT TO DO. WHEN HE LEARNT HOW IT WORKED AND MASTERED IT, IT WAS A DELIGHT TO USE.

I heard the Voice say...

"My Universe operates like a vast computer. Learn about it and master its Laws and your life will be a delight."

I SAT MAROONED ON THE ROCK ANXIOUSLY WAITING FOR THE INCOMING TIDE TO TURN. I THOUGHT IT WOULD NEVER DO SO AND I WOULD BE STUCK FOR EVER.

I heard the Voice say…

"Be patient. The tide of your fortunes will inevitably turn. Make sure you are ready when it does so."